FESTIVALS OF GOD

For the Congregation of God

2021

WATCHMEN OF GOD MINISTRIES

Daytona Beach fl

Festivals of God

For the Congregation of God

Author: Pastor Jose L Casillas

Index

A Welcome from Our Author:

God Bless and Shalom to ALL. I just wanted to thank you. and wish a Wonderful and Great Blessings on you and your Loved ones. It is my great pleasure and a warm welcome from the Casillas family and From

Our Lord and Savior Yahshua, with the guidance of The Holy Spirit and Our Heavenly Father Yahweh for touching your heart to get your hands on this Spiritual book. I promise it will open your spiritual eyes to see a new Horizon of in-depth look, on our spiritual growth towards Secrets that are Now, being revealed to the Children of God. It has been a stressful and hurtful experience to get this book out to you. The Child of God, to understand and hold dearly, that this is what God, wants All of us to do in our walk in the Faith. Thus, see us has part of the Body of Christ and has Citizens of Heaven and Part of Israel and its blessings, so with, thank you so much for buying this book, May the Blessings of Our Lord and Messiah Yahshua (Jesus) of Nazareth, the Son of Our God, Yahweh (Jehovah). May the Light always shine in your heart and be present, Always.

Author Jose L Casillas Crespo

Explaining the Importance of Gods Festivals

We are living in a world of deception and chaos without a doubt. The enemy for many decades has been conspiring and putting in action in bringing God's children under God's anger and displeasement with his Church on Earth and their wrongful practice of Idolatry without the Knowledge of His commandments in his holy scripture. Well, let me state a fact, we are in the last days and the enemy has erased the understanding of how important these festivals are to him (God). We are in drafted Into the Olive tree to where God has chosen people of many nationalities to make the Jewish people jealous so that they may seek him and call for him to come. This is a mandate toward me and you to practice what Our Lord and Savior to open the eyes of Our Jewish brother s to accept Yahshua (Jesus) as the true Messiah, in which he already came, and they did not know him. Thus, bring us to this question, why are we not practicing what God told us to do?

Zechariah 8:19

"Thus, says the **Lord of hosts**, 'The fast of the fourth, the fast of the fifth, the fast of the seventh and the fast of the tenth months will become joy, gladness, and cheerful feasts for the house of Judah; so, **love truth and peace**.'

Leviticus 23:2

Speak unto the children of Israel, and say unto them, **Concerning the feasts of the LORD**, which ye shall proclaim to be **holy convocations**, even these are <u>**my feasts**</u>.

Leviticus 23:4 These are the **feasts of the LORD**, even holy convocations, which ye shall proclaim in their seasons.

Numbers 10:10

And in the day of your gladness, and in your set feasts, and in your new moons, ye shall blow with the trumpets over your burnt-offerings and over your sacrifices of peace-offering; **and they shall be to you for a memorial before your God**: **I am Yahweh (Jehovah) your God**.

Matt 23:6

And love the uppermost **rooms at feasts**, and the chief seats in the synagogues,

These are just a few verses from different parts of the Holy Scriptures and how God himself is talking about these festivals. Ok, now with this freshly in your mind, can you ask yourself why us as the Children and disciples of Yahshua (Jesus) do not have these festivals in our churches? Also, even the fact why we do not even mention Israel in our prayers in churches or out of them in an assembly of any kind? Keep that in mind I will get back to it in a moment. Let us consider going into a church and they are celebrating for example a Christmas party, a Valentine assembly or any worldly assembly that is not instructed by the Holy Bible. I assure you this in Gods eyes is a disrespect and Angers him Greatly, second our spiritual leaders will be held accountable in these events. Even if we are eating in a room away by the main worship room in Gods eyes it is still considered in his House of Worship as an Offense to him as well. Just to be clear, if we are together holding an event or participating in a traditional practice of the world, using the Lord's house, can we agree that we are all responsible just as our spiritual leaders are? Apparently to answer this question in a more profound and clear answer. I will take you to verse.

1 Corinthians 10:20 On the contrary, the things which the Gentiles (pagans) sacrifice, they sacrifice to demons [in effect], and not to God; and I do not want you to become partners with demons [by eating at feasts in pagan temples]. I apologize if this may seem harsh, but, the true reality if a

Christian practice any type of celebration, event, party or gathering in the Church of God or temple is not permitted in his Holy Scriptures. This is considered a pagan practice in Our Lords eyes and is prohibited and frowned upon by God.

Jeremiah 10:1-4

Hear the word that the LORD speaks to you, O house of Israel. Thus, says the LORD: "**Learn not the way of the nations**, nor be dismayed at the signs of the heavens because the nations are dismayed at them, for the **customs of the peoples are vanity**. A tree from the forest is cut down and worked with an axe by the hands of a craftsman. They decorate it with silver and gold; they fasten it with hammer and nails so that it cannot move. Look, at how clearly this is referring to Christmas Holiday.

When you read the whole chapter, Idolatry caused thousands of Israelites to die in the desert for their pagan practice. The difference now, our Holy Spirit is being restricted from entering our place of worship, because even the Holy Spirit cannot dwell in a worship of idols it offends him as well. He is part of God, the Father and the Son. Thus, with it is an offense to him. The devil and the demons know if the church of God practice these unholy or unpermitted practices in our place of worship we are in big trouble with God. Especially the Spiritual leader permitting this in the House of the Lord. I did not say it, the Book of Life and Salvation did. It is of high importance I speak truth and not lie to you my brothers and sisters of the Faith. I love and pray for all my brothers and sisters of the Faith of our Lord Yahshua (Jesus) and I want them to enjoy the fruits of a Holy and fulfilled way of life. So, when they go up to see Our Lord face to face there is no blemish on our Pure white garments given to us by Yahshua (Jesus) in heaven. The devil wants us to practice everything of the world so we may be enemy s of God. Look at this verse **James 4:4.**

Ye adulterers and adulteresses, know ye not that **the friendship of the world is enmity with God**? **whosoever therefore will be a friend of the world is the enemy of God.** You see this a bold statement that James is saying that the Conduct of a Child of God should not be in any type of practice that is not considered correct in the eyes of the

Lord. Many believers of the faith are totally ignorant to these verses or really have not been taught that a practice other than what God has stated in his word is not rewarded and is an offense to the Lord. James is talking bluntly calling anyone who practices such things is an adulterer or adulteress. In the spiritual eyes, he is saying you have cheated on your God with another god other than the Highest. God does not see these as a practice but a betrayal! We must understand that God is a Jealous God and does not want his children serving another God in his name. When We relate to this understanding, this must bring us back to the time when Israel made a Gold Calf and worshiped it in God's name. Well, that caused thousands of Israelites to die for that great disrespect to the All Mighty, and many Christians are dying as we speak spiritually. Any pastor, leader of any congregation that tributes and financial gain with Christmas, thanksgiving or Mother's Day or Father's Day events are going to make a financial gain. So, with that in mind will consider these events godly and will speak highly of them and not negative, so that many will continue to attend those events in mention. It is harsh reality but, it is true.

The Importance of Christians Practice

Leviticus 23:2

The **feasts of the Lord**, which you shall **proclaim to be holy convocations**, these are **My feasts**" (Leviticus 23:2). Here God Almighty says in Scripture that these are His feasts. Why are they important to Him? And why should they be important to every Christian? Let us analyze this scripture verse, word for word. The first speaks of the Feasts of the Lord. Stop and think God is saying feasts a celebration. A feast is when you enjoy with family and friends the purpose and enjoy yourself with loved ones. Second feasts of the LORD, it is not just any feast, it has an owner the Lord Your God. Amazing!!!! This cannot be any clearer, has day and night. Also understand this, which you, shall proclaim. When you read this more than once, see how God is telling you to proclaim to be a HOLY convocation. Ok what does proclaim you might ask yourself.

Definition of proclaim (Google Word Definition)

verb: proclaim; 3rd person present: proclaims; past tense: proclaimed; past participle: proclaimed; gerund or present participle: proclaiming.

announce officially or **publicly**.

declare something one considers important with due emphasis.

"she proclaimed that what I had said was untrue."

declare officially or publicly to be.

"he proclaimed James II as King of England."

Also, when you see the definition of proclaim, you are not just saying this is a festival no you are announcing this is important in my life and it is officially and publicly important in my way of Life. Keep in mind this is a bold statement of your conviction of who you serve and why. Its pure (Holy) and Convocation (Assembly or a gather of people). You see not only are you proclaiming it, but it is considered in Gods eyes has something pure meaning, not a practice of vanity, but of Sanctification. Also, and an assembly of people with a bold statement has the Children of God.

Screaming in way of action, we are gathering here together for OUR GOD!!! with that said "Does this look like a feast of the Jews or a Feast mandated by Our living God? So, with this said, the questions of why we should see the importance of these feasts is because Our Lord mandated it, because they are his. Now let us look at the book of Exodus shall we.

Exodus 12

12 The Lord said to Moses and Aaron in
Egypt, 2 "**This month is to be for you** the first
month, the first month of your year. 3 Tell the
whole **community of Israel that on the tenth day
of this month each man is to take a lamb**[a] **for his
family, one for each household**. 4 If any household
is too small for a whole lamb, they must share one
with their nearest neighbor, having considered the
number of people there are. You are to determine
the amount of lamb needed in accordance with
what each person will eat. 5 The animals you
choose must be **year-old males without
defect**, and you may take them from the sheep or
the goats. 6 Take care of them until the fourteenth
day of the month, when all the members of the

community of Israel must slaughter them at twilight. [7]Then they are to take some of the blood and put it on the sides and tops of the doorframes of the houses where they eat the lambs. [8]That same night they are to eat the meat roasted over the fire, along with bitter herbs, and bread made without yeast. [9]Do not eat the meat raw or boiled in water but roast it over a fire—with the head, legs and internal organs. [10]Do not leave any of it till morning; if some is left till morning, you must burn it. [11]This is how you are to eat it: with your cloak tucked into your belt, your sandals on your feet and your staff in your hand. Eat it in haste; **it is the Lord's Passover.** This is in the Old Testament, but it talks about what is to come and who it will represent in the time to come. This is known as Passover and unleavened bread Feast. This is such a memorable and especially Important feast that All believers of Our Lord and Savior Yahshua (Jesus) should be part of their life. This is confirmed in the New testament a direct mention by John the Baptist speaking of Yahshua (Jesus). Who is the sacrificial Lamb of God? Let us see what John says. 1 John 29 The next day he saw Jesus coming towards him and declared, 'Here is the

Lamb of God who takes away the sin of the world! John speaks of Yahshua (Jesus) as The Lamb of God, which means he will be sacrificed for the sake of man. Mostly any reference you see of a sacrificial lamb in the old testament speaks of a sacrifice for someone's sin. The only difference is it only covered the sin does not erase it in front of God. Most of the arguments with theologians and scholars is we do not have to celebrate these festivals, because they were only for the Jews. Well, let me tell you I beg to differ, look at what Yahshua (Jesus) say about that argument. We will get the answer in this verse Luke22:19,20. "And he took bread, gave thanks and broke it, and gave it to them, saying, 'This is my body given for you; **do this in remembrance of me**.' In the same way, after the supper he took the cup, saying, 'This cup is the new covenant in my blood, which is poured out for you'" Now he is giving his disciples a command. Ok, with that said, read the second verse, after the supper. They had supper, isn't supper a full meal? Yes, it is, not only did he have an instruction to partake this Holy Festival but also telling them I am your sacrificial lamb. See, before it was a practice to remember this

Festival due to the Exodus of Egypt of its hard and long-awaited freedom from the slavery of Egypt's Pharaoh. In this fashion what Israel remembered. but now Yahshua (Jesus) is saying I Am Your Passover and Unleavened bread. Now, when you have Passover, you are to remember Me, that is what he was saying with authority. View these festivals has a confirmation of your faith and worship to Our living God Yahshua (Jesus) and his victory over death and the gates of hell. He is our Passover our All, before the end of this book the Holy Spirit will convict you in these festivals and you will have a New understanding of these wonderful festivals and what they should mean to you and you will have a vail opening over your eyes. God does not do anything without a purpose of reason. Yes, the Older brothers, the Jewish people practice it but, it was shown to them by God not by any other way or reason. If you read the old testament in their travel to the promise land they were guided and instructed by God himself. He mandated them all to practice these Festivals, just a representation of what to come.

I would like to put an emphasis in these scripture verses to give you a clear understanding of how important it is to obey God's word and to practice what he says to do. Many Christians fail to understand let alone practice this type of obedience due to lack of knowledge and how it will affect their spiritual growth and what ministry God wants to come out of his children. See, we all have a Ministry in Gods eyes and with obedience with God he will open doors and send his servants to reveal what is your calling. Let us see this verse.

1 Samuel 15:22 "And Samuel said, "Has the Lord as great delight in burnt offerings and sacrifices, as in obeying the voice of the Lord? Behold, to obey is better than sacrifice, and to listen than the fat of rams."

Genesis 22:18 "and in your offspring shall all the nations of the earth be blessed, because you have obeyed my voice."

Isaiah 1:19 "If you are willing and obedient, you shall eat the good of the land."

Romans 6:16 "Do you not know that if you present yourselves to anyone as obedient slaves, you are slaves of the one whom you obey, either of sin, which leads to death, or of obedience, which leads to righteousness?"

Joshua 1:7 "Be strong and very courageous. Be careful to obey all the law my servant Moses gave you; do not turn from it to the right or to the left, that you may be successful wherever you go."

In a time of exceptionally low respect of the House of God, were many have allowed (spiritual Leaders) from disco tech lights, theatrical dances, even smoke boxes to give an affect or even the practice of mimicking in churches with Christian music, making a Temple of the Lord a worldly spectacle. Only, shows me that these Leaders that allow such actions in Gods Church is an act of disobedience with God's commandments of Holiness in His temple and inside our human bodies which in Gods eyes is as well a temple of the Lord were the Holy Spirit resides. Even the most commandments of scripture are Ten Commandments. The highest is watching every move of his children on earth, and he sees most of them not obeying him in his scripture. I would like for you to understand what scripture speaks about when a prophet of

God would appear. Mainly to bring the people of back from there sin and wrongful practice of living. Now, most of these so-called prophets of God only prophecies prosperity and good fortune. If you see a prophet of God saying these things run, he is lying and not doing what God uses these prophets for, to bring his children back from wrongdoing in Our Lords eyes. Why, you might ask why I mentioned prophets. Well, because normally when a congregation is starting to fall away from the Lord's sanctification lifestyle is because some prophesied some words to the congregation and then they fall or fail to keep themselves away from ill practice and which is a deception from the devil.

1 John 4:1-6

Beloved, do not believe every spirit, but test the spirits to see whether they are from God, for many false prophets have gone out into the world. By this you know the Spirit of God: every spirit that confesses that Jesus Christ has come in the flesh is from God, and every spirit that does not confess Jesus is not from God. This is the spirit of the antichrist, which you heard was coming and now is in the world already. Little children, you are from God and have overcome them, for he who is in you is greater than he who is in the world. They are from the world; therefore, they speak from the world, and the world listens to them.

Jeremiah 14:14

And the LORD said to me: "The prophets are prophesying lies in my name. I did not send them, nor did I command them or speak to them. They are prophesying to you a lying vision, worthless divination, and the deceit of their own minds.

These two verses are exactly what is going on in these mega churches, people prophesying lies and leading people away from God's obedience and his holy practices which he wants his children to practice. Most of these types of spiritual leaders gain financial gain from leading you astray from what God wants and what they want the congregation of God to do in this world. Since, we are in the Last Days before the coming of Christ Return. The Holy Bible speaks noticeably clear of what not to be deceived. Which, sadly to say is exactly what is going on in many churches today.

Why is it Important to change our old customs?

Titus 2:12 Training us to renounce ungodliness and worldly passions, and to live self-controlled, upright, and godly lives in the present age,

Colossians 3:5

Put to death therefore what is earthly in you: sexual immorality, impurity, passion, evil desire, and covetousness, which is idolatry.

Luke 16:13

No servant can serve two masters, for either he will hate the one and love the other, or he will be devoted to the one and despise the other. You cannot serve God and money."

I wanted to emphasis with these three verses. Due to the Bible extensive Bible verses and stories in change I felt these were clear and very to the point. When we go to Christ, we are slowly but surely in a time of change. All our habits that we had when we were in the world practicing sin. We were self-centered human beings and did not care about change; it was I want to do this, so I did it. We basically lived our lives conformity of what we wanted, or any type of influence just guided us to do what our hearts were content to do. According, to our behaviors or who we associated with, that is what we would do. But now that we seek truth and serve our Lord with Our lives, we let God change us through scripture and spiritual lectures, preaching, worship and so on. I have noticed that when we start for the first years of serving the Lord, we want dramatic change in our lives. Which that is great! Of course, we want that and so does God. He wants us to be Holy Spirit filled and reading the Bible, word of Life, but he also wants us to change our traditional behavior has well. Look at this verse.

Colossians 2:8

See to it that no one takes you captive by philosophy and empty. deceit, according to human tradition, according to the elemental spirits of the world, and not according to Christ.

Many spiritual speakers or Leaders due to their theology courses and certificates and fancy names or titles, can persuade people to make them believe that what they are saying by just listening to them and can slowly guide you away from what God wants you to do and this is the danger of these men. Let me explain any man or women who tries to persuade you to continue a practice that you did when you were in the world, to Now, that you are serving the Lord and keeping you in a practice not commanded by God is leading you to a human traditional practice. Changing in God's presence is not doing the same things you did when you were in the world. That also includes, changing your traditional practice, meaning any traditional practice you did, should change also. God. Has many wonderful and spiritual traditions, that were mandated by him, and commands us to practice them, because, they have spiritual growth that can affect our lives. This is what this book is all about opening your spiritual eyes to a new traditional practice of Holy festivals that will bless you and your family and give you a more profound look of who God is and how wonderful his feast is a new Life changing life in Christ. Not, practicing the same man traditions that the world continues to practice that are nothing but vain. Sometimes, I am flabbergasted, by how the churches practice pagan holidays or holidays that are worldly and have no place in God's house. All these festivals, that the world practice traditional and faithfully are nothing, but, a financial gain, for the Pastors, spiritual leaders that want you to think it is Ok, to keep- these practices and you will still be rewarded by God. I can honestly say with full conviction that it is incorrect, and a danger to every Christians spiritual growth.

What are the Consequences on Not Obeying God?

Most of the brothering in Christ forget one thing. The importance of obeying God in this time is most important. No other philosophies of other scripture base concept of thinking are not going to come into favor with the Lord. We were created for him and only him and no man cannot afford to be in Gods angered eye. His scripture has so much warning's in not obeying his word and look what happened to Israel for trying to worship him in a disrespectful behavior in the Almighty. There is a story of Moses setting aside those who chose God and those who chose the way of Korah,Dathan and Abiram who wanted to go back to Egypt. Those that chose Moses, lived and those that followed man's ways, the Earth opened and swallowed them whole. It is in the book of

Numbers 16:20-35.

The LORD said to Moses and Aaron, "Move away from these men! I want to destroy them now!" But Moses and Aaron bowed to the ground and cried out, "God, you know what people are thinking. Please do not be angry with all these people. Only one man really sinned." Then the LORD said to Moses, "Tell the people to move away from the tents of Korah, Dathan, and Abiram." Moses stood and went to Dathan and Abiram. All the elders of Israel followed him. Moses warned the people, "Move away from the tents of these evil men. Do not touch anything that belongs to them! If you do, you will be destroyed because of their sins." So, the men moved away from the tents of Korah, Dathan, and Abiram. Dathan and Abiram went to their tents. They stood outside of their tents with their wives, children, and little babies. Then Moses said, "I will show you proof that the LORD sent me to do all the things I told you. I will show you that all these things were not my own idea. These men will die, but if they die in a normal way—the way people always die—then that will show that the LORD did not really send me. But if the LORD causes them to die in a different way, then you will know that these men have sinned against the causes them to die in a different way, then you will know that these men have sinned against the LORD. This is the proof: The earth will open and swallow them. They will go down to their grave still alive. And everything that belongs to these men will go down with them." When Moses finished saying these things, the ground under the men opened. It was as if the earth opened its mouth and swallowed them. All Korah's men, their families, and everything they owned went down into the earth. They went down into their grave alive. Everything they owned went with them. Then the earth closed over them. They were finished—gone from the camp! The Israelites heard the cries of the men being destroyed. So, they all ran in different directions and said, "The earth will swallow us too!" Then a fire came from the LORD and destroyed the 250 men who were offering the incense. This is your perfect example of Disobedience to God his Commandments and way of Living only to him. Yes, we all free will but that is between your choices with what will be for disobedience. Following Christ is based on fasting and prayer no other way. You must relate to The Holy Spirit and you will be set free from all captivity in the Spirit. Our God is a spiritual base God who wishes only your spiritual well and being of Health. Lack of taking care of yourself and your relationship with God is at stake if this is not your Goal to please your God.

What does God say about Traditional Festivals and His festivals?
Versus on Human practices handed for Traditional vs God?

Colossians 2:8

See to it that no one takes you captive by philosophy and empty deceit, according to human tradition, according to the elemental spirits of the world, and not according to Christ.

Mark 7:13

Thus, making void the word of God by your tradition that you have handed down. And many such things you do."

Mark 7:8

You leave the commandment of God and hold to the tradition of men."

Mathew 15:6

he need not honor his father.' So, for the sake of your tradition, you have made void the word of God.

Here is your other example of how the Disciples of Christ were speaking of things being seen with Their own eyes and blaming their actions on Traditional ways of Man. There is no necessary explaining of these versus they are truth. So now we will go to the Festivals of God.

Holy Festivals and What they Are.

1. Pesach – The Passover
2. Yom Kippur – Day of atonement
3. Hanukkah-Festival of Light, Festival of Dedication
4. Rosh Hashanah -New Year
5. Shemini Atzaret-Rejoicing Torah (The Word of God)
6. Shavuot – Feast of week or Pentecost
7. Sukkot = Feast of Tabernacle

These are but the Most Important Holiday a Christian should practice and are allowed by Christ, Himself, and spoke of these festivals, you shall practice. Yahshua is telling all his followers I did these things because they are mines and my Fathers. Most of these festivals if not all are an opening yourself to a spiritual life. Not a flesh but of uplifting and closeness with God. You are to do these things in order as they were established by God himself. These are not the Jews festivals but of God. I cannot stress that more strongly. These festivals guide you to the Life of a Child of God, not of this world. You will understand more the word and its application to your life. Not a practice or tradition but of life essence to get close to your creator and owner. Plain and Simple.

The Passover old and New

The Passover in the old view is the Image of a sheep being sacrificed for the Covering of the sin of that individual or family. It was to come to be a Human sacrifice of the Divine Prophesy foretold many ages ago of a Messiah. Which in this very moment many Jews have rejected the concept of Jesus of Nazareth being him. Although the prophecy did say his own people will reject him and will not know him. That is in the book of Lucas. When Jesus died on the cross, he became our Sacrificial Lamb and Now he is to be remembered on The Festival of Passover. Jesus passed us over from damnation to Salvation.

The Command to observe Passover is found in Exodus 12.

The LORD said to Moses and Aaron in Egypt, "This month is to be for you the first month, the first month of your year. Tell the whole community of Israel that on the tenth day of this month each man is to take a lamb for his family, one for each household... That same night they are to eat the meat roasted over the fire, along with bitter herbs, and bread made without yeast... Eat it in haste; it is the LORD's Passover." (Exodus 12:1-3, 8, 11

Here is the Explanation of Passover

Once a year, Jews devote an entire week to recalling the events of the Exodus, internalizing these messages, and growing in their faith. One way they do this is through the ritual Passover meal known as the *seder*, which is the heart of the Passover celebration. At the *seder* meal, the *Haggadah* is read. This is the text that has been used for all of these generations to guide the *seder*, saying: "For God did not redeem our ancestors alone, but us, as well. The unleavened bread also symbolizes Yahshua (Jesus). Meaning he had no sin, which the yeast symbolize sin as well. This is also eaten in the Passover meal.

Yom Kippur: The Day of Atonement

Leviticus 16:29 mandates establishment of this holy day on the 10th day of the 7th month as the day of atonement for sins. It calls it the Sabbath of Sabbaths and a day upon which one must afflict one's soul. Leviticus 23:27 decrees that **Yom Kippur** is a strict day of rest. **Yom Kippur**—the Day of Atonement—is considered the most important holiday in the Jewish faith. ... According to tradition, it is on **Yom Kippur** that God decides each person's fate, so Jews are encouraged to make amends and ask forgiveness for sins, committed during the past year. Not only was it mandated by God to his people, but to All that serve him in truth. Everyone that follows the ways of Our Lord in scripture and in life living sacrifice to do what, The Lord ordained us to follow his Festival is crucial in knowing who God is in your life.

Hanukkah: Festival of Lights *Hanukkah,* also known as the Festival of Lights or the Festival of Dedication, is a celebration for the Jewish people. *Hanukkah* lasts eight days and falls sometime in late November or December, close to the Christian celebration of Christmas. (On the Hebrew calendar, *Hanukkah* begins on the 25th day of the month of *Kislev*). Customs like lighting the *menorah* reveal the deeper themes of the holiday, such as hope, light, and miracles. Unlike some Jewish holidays when Jews are instructed not to do any work, Jews can go to work and school during this festival. Since Hebrew and English use different alphabets and there is no set standard for converting one alphabet to another when translating, *Hanukkah* can be spelled various ways, including *Chanukah*.

When you look at this Festival is speaking about hope in your Lord, a better understanding that he Is the Light of the World. In John 8:12 **Jesus** applies the title to himself while debating with the Jews and states: I am the **light of the world**. Whoever follows me will never walk in darkness but will have the **light** of life. Knowing this and practicing this festival in everyday living will bring you closer than ever before to who you follow and practice the Light of the World Yahushua (Jesus).

Rosh Hashanah The New Year of Gods Children

Now, I know you have heard and even practiced, Worldly New Year's Eve, but, if you Worship the True and Living God. This is your True Celebration of New Year. You see the Bible is not by any other Calendar than the Hebrew Calendar. There is a reason a time and place and season for everything that is Celebrated in Gods Festivals. *Rosh Hashanah*, the Jewish New Year, is observed on the first day of the month of *Tishrei* on the Hebrew calendar, which falls in September or October on the Gregorian calendar (the calendar in common use throughout the world).

Unlike the secular New Year, *Rosh Hashanah* (which means, literally, "the head of the year" in English) is not characterized by frivolity and celebration. Instead, it is a holy day marked by intense moral and spiritual introspection. On this day, children of God consider themselves plaintiffs appealing for their lives before, the Supreme Judge and Ruler of the universe.

Because of this judgment, the mood pervading *Rosh Hashanah* is one of solemnity—but it is also one of trust in a God who is a merciful and beneficent Father, desires our repentance, and is eager to grant forgiveness. In the words of the prophet Ezekiel:

"But if a wicked man turns away from all the sins he has committed and keeps all my decrees and does what is just and right, he will surely live; he will not die. . .. Do I take any pleasure in the death of the wicked? declares the Sovereign LORD. Rather, am I not pleased when they turn from their ways and live? . . . Rid yourselves of all the offenses you have committed and get a new heart and a new spirit." — Ezekiel 18:21, 23, 31

Jewish sages teach that fates are "written" as God judges the world on *Rosh Hashanah* and "sealed" ten days later *Yom Kippur*, the Day of Atonement and the holiest day on the Hebrew calendar. The period in between the two holy days is known as the Ten Days of Repentance, or the Days of Awe, during which reflection and penitence intensify.

Jews know they are judged by their actions during the whole year, but just as one would be that much more careful while sitting in a courtroom in front of the presiding judge, they know that now is their last chance to make good before the King of

Kings, the Judge of Judges—God Himself—before His judgment is made.

Of course, this spirit of humility and reconciliation is to follow Jews throughout the year, throughout their lives. But the High Holy Days are when Jews believe that they have the most power to transform themselves and channel their abilities and resources to serve God.

Just as the secular New Year invites introspection on the past 12 months and resolutions for the year to come, so too, the Jewish New Year calls for examination of past mistakes and planning for improvement in the future. Not only is this so important in our lives but it is a reflection practice of what was done the year prior to how to better ourselves and show our wrong doings and how to practice this to better each other in God's word and practice. It is a way of self-checking and connecting yourself with truth in your actions but also in humbleness to yourself to know if in you do not better yourself in a looking yourself in the mirror action you will continue to stop a spiritual progress in your life. The word will refresh you and guide you to a better moral and character in Christ.

Shemini Atzaret- Rejoicing Torah (The Word of God)

Immediately following the joyous festival of *Sukkot,* Jews around the world celebrate the holidays of *Shemini Atzeret* and *Simchat Torah*. *Shemini Atzeret*, or the "Eighth Day of Assembly," is technically a holiday in its own right, though it is also connected to the festival of *Sukkot*: *"For seven days present food offerings to the LORD, and on the eighth day hold a sacred assembly"* (Leviticus 23:36). In Israel, these two celebrations occur on the same day, but in the diaspora, *Shemini Atzeret* is celebrated immediately after *Sukkot* ends.

Shemini Atzeret marks the end of one of the most intense, inspirational, and celebratory seasons on the Jewish calendar, known as the High Holy Days. The journey began with *Rosh Hashanah*, Judgment Day, followed by *Yom Kippur*, the Day of Atonement, and then we marked *Sukkot* with seven festive days. Now, it is time to return to "regular life."

In explaining the meaning of this holiday, one rabbinic parable compared God to a human king whose children come to visit him in the capital only three times a year. The king, enjoying their company so much and being so saddened by their departure, bids them to stay on an extra day. Similarly, God so loves His children, the people of Israel, and is so pleased that they have come to the Temple in Jerusalem to celebrate the festival, that He has difficulty "parting" with them. He, therefore, bids them to stay an additional day.

Shemini Atzeret is a day of transition – from the excitement and anticipation of the High Holy Days to the routine of daily life. It is also the day that connects the High Holy Days to the rest of the year. It is the day on which God seemingly says, "Don't leave it all behind – take the inspiration of these days back into your lives."

Now we can understand why Jews then celebrate the *Torah* on *Simchat Torah,* which immediately follows *Shemini Atzeret.* God's Word is the vehicle through which holiness is infused into daily life. The holiday also underscores the centrality of the *Torah* to Jewish life, as both a source of Jewish identity and a gift from God. It is the one day on which the entire community gathers to express joy together for having received God's Word.

This festival, which originated in the Middle Ages, marks the completion of the annual cycle of reading from the *Torah*. Each week in synagogue, Jews read a portion of the *Torah,* called the *parshah.* **You can follow along with these readings with Yael Eckstein's daily Holy Land Moments devotions.** Throughout the year, Jews annually read from the beginning chapter of Genesis to the final chapter in Deuteronomy. Then a huge party breaks out! Except for *Purim*, *Simchat Torah* is the most joyous festival on the Jewish calendar. A perfect example of The Festival of God not only brings his word has a recognition of Gods power in the life of a Human being but also a Festival of Rejoicing in Gods written word and God himself Yahshua (Jesus) being the word in Life. What an amazing Festival that speaks of Our Living God.

Shavuot – Feast of week or Pentecost

Shavuot is a Gods holiday that commemorates the single most important event in Israel's history: the giving of the *Torah* (the first five books in the Hebrew Bible) to Moses at Mount Sinai. Although it is not as well known among non-Jews as Passover or *Sukkot,* the Feast of Booths, it is one of the three major festivals often called "pilgrim" festivals because all Jewish males were required to observe them at the Holy Temple in Jerusalem.

More than 3,000 years ago, after leaving Egypt on the night of Passover, the Jews traveled to the Sinai desert. There, they experienced divine revelation as God gave the Jewish people His Law.

In Deuteronomy 4:10–13, Moses reminded the people of that experience:

"Remember the day you stood before the Lord your God at Horeb [Sinai] . . . You came near and stood at the foot of the mountain while it blazed with fire to the very heavens, with black clouds and deep darkness. Then the Lord spoke . . . He declared to you his covenant, the Ten Commandments, which he commanded you to follow and then wrote them on two stone tablets."

Shavuot is the culmination of the seven weeks between Passover and the giving of the Law. Indeed, the very term *Shavuot* means "weeks." Since *Shavuot* occurs 50 days after the first day of Passover, it is sometimes known as Pentecost, which is a Greek word that means "fifty." Jesus' followers were in Jerusalem celebrating Pentecost when the Holy Spirit was given to them, and so, many churches today celebrate Pentecost as the birth of the church.

The two holidays, Passover and *Shavuot*, are linked by more than just their proximity. The Exodus from Egypt, which Passover celebrates, marked the beginning of physical freedom for the Jewish people. But *Shavuot* is a reminder for the Jews that physical liberation was incomplete without the spiritual redemption represented by receiving God's law. *Shavuot* is also called *Atzeret,* meaning "the completion," because together with Passover it forms the completion of a unit. Jews gained their freedom from Egypt on Passover in order to receive the *Torah* on *Shavuot*.

The earlier celebrations of *Shavuot* were more agricultural in nature and motif. In ancient times, sheaves of barley (the winter crop) were brought to the Temple each day, starting on Passover until *Shavuot,* the beginning of the harvesting season 50 days later. Farmers looked forward to *Shavuot* with great anticipation. When it finally arrived, the people would bring their first fruits to the Temple amid great pomp and ceremony. They rejoiced before God and thanked Him for their material blessings.

With the destruction of the Second Temple and the forced separation of the Jewish people from their land, the centrality of the harvest motif diminished. Instead, the theme of the anniversary of the revelation of the *Torah* to Moses on Mount Sinai gained dominance—a theme continued today.

Many Jews today celebrate *Shavuot* by staying up the entire night studying and learning the *Torah*. At synagogue services on *Shavuot* morning, the Ten Commandments are read, and the people reaffirm their commitment to treasure and obey God's Law. According to a well-known Jewish *Midrash* (the oral traditions that eventually were written down), God initially offered the *Torah* to each of 70 nations, who would not accept it without first asking what it was about. After hearing the commandments, each nation had some excuse for not accepting them. God finally turned to the nation of Israel, who said *"kol asher diber Adonai na'aseh,"* which means "all that the LORD says we will do." Unlike the other nations, Israel chose the *Torah* before knowing its contents (Exodus 19:8).

Today, after the reading of the Ten Commandments during *Shavuot*, Jews reaffirm their commitment to God, to the *Torah*, and to their faith, by repeating those same words: "All that the LORD says we will do."

Sukkot: The Feast of Tabernacle

Sukkot is a weeklong Jewish holiday that comes five days after Yom Kippur. Sukkot celebrates the gathering of the harvest and commemorates the miraculous protection G-d provided for the children of Israel when they left Egypt. We celebrate Sukkot by dwelling in a foliage-covered booth (known as a *sukkah*).

The first two days (sundown on October 2 until nightfall on October 4 in of the holiday (one day in Israel) are Yom, when work is forbidden, candles are lit in the evening, and festive meals are preceded by Kiddush and include challah dipped in honey.

The intermediate days (nightfall on October 4 until sundown on October 9 in are quasi holidays, known as Chol HaMoed. We dwell in the *sukkah* and take the Four Kinds every day of

Sukkot (except for Shabbat, when we do not take the Four Kinds).

The final two days (sundown on October 10 until nightfall on October 11 are a separate holiday (one day in Israel): Shemini Atzeret / Simchat Torah.

Here you have brother s and Sisters of the Faith. These are but a few of what God has to offer and how these Festivals can enrich your spiritual life. Now to make sure you understand that these Festivals are of God. As you know our older brothers the Jews practice these, yes. But to emphasis the important quote of all. These are God's festivals not the Jews. These were given to Moses for the Jews to have a heavenly connection with God! All these Festivals has you already read and seen for yourself they have meaning. Worldly Festivals have a hidden agenda belief and are older than you think and are what they are, ways of worshiping another god, not the one you serve or believe to serve. These Festivals nourish your spiritual growth and bind you more with the Holy Spirit and Our Wonderful and Great and Living God.

Why is it so Important to make these Festivals part of our lives?

I will not place to much emphasis on this matter but I had to include this chapter so you may understand that these Festivals are so much important in the Christian living. You cannot help to think the day you accepted your lord and Savior in your life and in your family and in your home. You made a commitment to yourself and to your loved ones to know all it is to know about the God you serve. When you do this type of research it is crucial your aware that you are entering in the domain of the Highest. God does not do anything without reason and these Festivals will still be celebrated when God restores the World to its original creation and reason to be. With that being said that means they are important in a Christian living because you will continue this even when you are brought to heaven for a short period of time and The New Jerusalem will be brought down from heaven to the New Rebuilt Earth to be here forever and ever. I am revealing to you a heavenly secret that was shown to me and I am sharing it with you the reader to understand. How important you are in Gods eyes and how you are a citizen of Heaven and part of Israel as well! These Festivals were created by God for you and Israel. Why? You might ask yourself because Sanctification means to be A part of something. In this case is God giving you a new way of life, a New way of celebration life through his Festivals and Glorifying his name constantly. He is the Alpha and Omega; he is the Beginning and the End. He should be your all, your purpose of Living and purpose of celebration this is exactly what All Jews do! They place their entire life in servitude to God but let us be honest not all are or have accepted the True Messiah, Yahushua (Jesus). So many do it in a traditional way, many even practices this as such a Tradition, many do not even know why they do it, they just do. So, with that in mind You are in a better place than them because you are going to do it for the Love of His Son Yahshua (Jesus). So, what better gift to give your father in heaven and acknowledging God the father and His Amazing Son and the Holy Spirit in such a way you not only worship him in the Church but also in your life practice and binding yourself with Israel and Celebrating these beautiful Festivals and teaching others there is more than just going to church. It is an amazing thought to understand that you can have so many conversations with Festivals and supernatural experience uniting your family in such a heaven filled celebration. When in doubt whether it is important or not this is what the Devil has done so much in his war against all that love God, to eradicate Gods beautiful festivals out of church and to eliminate it out of your Christian Life so that you will not experience a stronger relationship with God Almighty. Remember the Job of Lucifer is to destroy you and keep you has far away from the Truth and practice of committing your entire life to God and his Commandments and ordinances that are still alive and well in these perilous times. Let us restart our Life with God and start to enjoy these Festivals that will bring you Joy.

How the Devil has managed to eliminate these Holy

Festivals out of the Churches of God.

Since the beginning of time that devil has always hated God creation Man. In his eyes (the devil) we are nothing, but dogs and should be destroyed. When lucifer was kicked out of heaven he did not go alone he was thrown down from heaven with a third of angels. Which are now considered the fallen angels or known as demons. We must understand that this battle we have is not with human beings, meaning flesh in blood but of Spiritual Warfare. As we continue to investigate further understanding of what the world is trying to tell us and what is the word trying to speak to us and there is a constant battle between you and God and the devil. Most of these festivals were created so the children of God have a purpose and have a spiritual understanding, and a revelation of who God is. the Old Testament books, the Five first books of the Bible. Give you reference to the characteristics of God, Yahshua (Jesus)and Holy Spirit. So, if we really tend to understand these things in a more spiritual aspect of not trying to look at a mental aspect without the guidance of the Holy Spirit most of these Gods festivals were so important that even still to this day, the majority of the Jews of Israel, are constantly practicing them so with that being in mind, why, can't we see being called the children of God. We continue to practice worldly traditions, worldly festivals, that in the background. They are very diabolical and are traditions and festivals, that are not related to God? I have come to understand that while I was studying the origin of Worldly Festivals have a hidden paganism worship of other gods. So, most of these festivals that we tend to look at really have no purpose in the church. Mainly, the worldly festivals ,are not meant for those that choose Christ ,these festivals of the world are mainly for the people that chose their daily living without Christ and are involved in their vain and selfish living. We as a congregation of God, we must understand that these festivals(Gods Festivals) have been eradicated for the purpose of you, not to have a deeper understanding of God. Which they were meant for Israel and you because if we don't study these festivals then guess what, we lose so much. Why, they were created to be a blessing to you! Why ? There meant for the children of God, so they can have a purpose , a meaningful festival, a sacred and holy festival, that only God ,is the owner and created it and it also, reminds you of all the wonderful and miraculous events that God did for the people of Israel which you are now involved. The enemy has been dealing with man for thousands and thousands of years he knows that even in his time he tried to eradicate the church, but, since he couldn't eradicate the church. He changed his plan, he infiltrated the church and changed the structure of worship and true knowledge ,so that instead of the church being a blessing it was pretty much being contaminated by worldly things and people are still following those traditions and still following that way of life, as a daily basis and totally ignoring that God sent to do these things. The reason why I put this chapter in this book is because what I want is the reader to understand that the festivals of God, they are of God, they are not of the Jews. They were giving to the Jews ,so that you may learn how to practice them. But they were also given to everyone that chose to serve God, chosen to serve the God of the Jews, which he is truly only one God, he is not a Trinity, like many of people are saying he is not a three people ,he is Only One God and One Only God, and you know they all work the same. God has always said it, he is the father, has always been considered the one God. He has always been considered the true and righteous God and powerful, the almighty. We must understand that we as children of God ,must understand, that we belong to him. If we tend to study the word more,and let the Holy Spirit make us understand the secrets in the Bible, we will get such an enriched understanding and know that these festivals are beautiful and have a deeper understanding of Who God and Yahshua(Jesus) is than we will know that these festivals, were meant for us. I constantly see and I constantly am wondering, why is it, that in all churches, they all practice the same thing, some practice Christmas some practice, Thanksgiving or change the name of Valentine's Day and instead of listening to what the word says when the word really tells you to practice Gods festivals and to stay away from the Pagan practices. It's like they(the Church)doesn't ask God if what they are doing is right or wrong. It's like they don't even think about it or they don't even tend to understand, what is God really telling us. God his son is telling us the Church of Christ stay away, from those festivals because they have a background that it has nothing to do with me and all you doing is a tradition that is basically destroying my commandments destroying my ordinances. Now, let me be plain let us, put ourselves in God shoes, if he ordained us to do something and we do not do it, are we under obedience, no we are not. We are constantly practicing something that has nothing to do with the Lord almighty we are constantly following what man, is teaching us, we do not even go question, what the pastor Says, because you must see if you are being led by someone, he must prove to you, that what he is doing is right in the eyes of the Lord ,according to the scripture, that has been given. This is where I go against all this theology and philosophy teachings or all the stories about people trying to bring in an understanding of philosophes and things that have to do with God and because of this educated college doctorate leader or pastor has the right to dictate that or this or this pastor has studied for so many years ,I must listen to him, No , if it doesn't concur with Biblical scripture ,I am not forced to listen or do what he or she says . I am obligated to do what Gods word says , period. It does not matter how many years you have in the gospel, or how much study you have in the gospel. If whatever you are doing, is not according to what God ordained us or commanded us to do, it is totally against God, and we must understand that as a children of God, Chapter Hosea, talks about this is, my people were destroyed for lack of knowledge. That is exactly what is going on in the in the congregations today. The congregation, rather have the pastor teach them what each story means. Instead of themselves putting themselves in prayer and fasting, and let the Holy Spirit tell them, what it means. My brothers and sisters, we are in a time, that we are so close to the Kingdom of heaven coming. We are so close to God picking up his church and we are not ready, and we are still doing what we feel like we want to do, and we are still going to do what we wish to do, sadly but surely that plane is going to leave us behind. I am writing this book so that I can illuminate, and guide as much as I can to have our brothers to think for themselves, to let the Holy Spirit guide them and bring them to the truth. Not to let us, act like census people that have no consciousness and are constantly letting ourselves be guided by the pastor or whatever leaders is in their church. a. Look at what is going on around the world, do we really think we are in the right course, to go to heaven? Sadly, but surely, we are not. Multiple people and millions of Christians are not totally against these festivals, but practice blindly, If you ask them their origin they don't have a clue. When you read the New Testament, you will see that before the coming of Christ, you will see in the book of Daniel 8 and Mathew 24 there it states, an abomination desolation to the altars of Churches, that is exactly what is going on right now. To where now a pulpit is a theatrical entrance and not a worship or message place,a lot of motivational speaking. I watch and I look at many YouTube videos and many sites you see in these big churches and megachurches a constant emotional motivational speaking type preaching. It is a lot of philosophy garbage hand me down Christian belief that really has no foundation of the good book itself. Let me explain, majority of these motivational speakers are so called preachers when you see that they mention more of mercy more of Grace not of redemption more of give God $1000 and I will give you $10,000 it is not in the gospel ,that's a gospel, that is cursed because, Paul, spoke about it ,and he said that if they were being taught, something other than what the Jesus taught the disciples, then it was a curse gospel. We must understand that in old Times. Now, which is called modern times, the old disciples, that followed the disciples of Christ in their time. Kept close attention to what the disciple were teaching and practiced it, they also kept away from what the worldly practice, they practiced mainly of what the Holy Spirit told them as well.They(old time Christians) Did not worry too much about philosophy, because at that time there was many people, especially the Greeks, that were people that were always on philosophy, so they knew exactly what that was. They also knew what a Pagan practice was, Because, at that time when the disciples of the old times were walking the earth, many practices were being done and were Pagan traditions handed down from father to son and so on. So, with all if you put it down and just one understanding. Stay away from Pagan practices, because they were not for the children of God and the children of God back in the those days did not practice Pagan practices,but in the New Testament Paul did right some letters scolding many believers for themselves fall so quickly to other people s teachings other than what they were taught by them.Although the old time Christians, they did practice the holy festival's given by Moses to the people of Israel. Which was given to Moses by God himself to give to his people, to show that they may remember, the miracles that God did in their lives. So, they can pass it down to generation and generation so they can realize that they knew that God was always with them and God would take them out of whatever situation they were because he knew that they were practicing what he ordained him to do. To practice the festivals, that he ordained, and not to practice the festivals from the world. That is why, it is crucial for the enemy to take away all these beautiful festivals, that were given to us by God, himself, so that we can be under damnation, in front of God. God will not bless us, that was why he, (Satan) erased the festivals of God, and took out all the understanding, from our Jewish older brothers, so that we will never understand, the beauty in the spiritual guidance of these festivals. Remember the devil does plan what he is going to do against the people of God. The enemy knows that these festivals are crucial for us to understand the people of Israel and to understand God himself. So, we must listen to the word and not listen to men, why because what good is it for us to listen to man than to listen to the almighty God and his word.

How Does Israel play such an Important part in Our lives?

It has come to my attention, that I realized about, Israel the Holy Land. It has been a controversial mentality that Israel is not important in Christian's life. What if we if we were to really understand what God was saying and how God chose these people that were under slavery and how symbolically how God for the illumination of what he has done in the time of crucifixion when he died for our sins it is so amazing for me to understand that he chose people that were enslaved and bonded by Egypt which is in in a spiritual sense we as well in the modern times were enslaved in normal living by just living a daily life without God in our hearts, and also living without God in our lives. So, when I think about Israel, I think about so many things. I have been thinking about the supernatural events, that happened in that continent, or as you can say in that special land, and how they are surrounded constantly by people that just want to harm them, and how it is so funny, when you realize that for it being such a small place and how God is still protecting Israel, and how God, kept his promise to them. I have no doubt in my mind, that once we fully understand that it is where every Christian person, is going to reign or live, which is Jerusalem. Jerusalem has so much culture and so much supernatural events that happened, and that is now, Israel has always been what we have read in the word of God, which is the Bible. But the Bible also is what we ask as believers in Yahshua (Jesus) are believers in God, but the Bible is really a history based written, real life events and how we really overlook that! So, we do not really see what the Bible really is, we keep reading the Bible and just keep reading the stories and how God is so amazing. So many things in life can get you used to reading a book and sometimes that all we see pages but not words written with power to change our lives. We see how many people and so many prophets and so much wisdom teachings are in the Bible, but yeah, we really do not understand that it was founded in Israel. It was founded on the Homeland, and that it was written in the Holy Land, where Yahshua or Jesus walked the earth, as a human being and was Christ, crucified and died. I am just so dumbfounded that a lot of Christians do not even think about our Jewish brothers and do not think about all the wisdom and knowledge that they have from centuries and decades of being under such a powerful wonderful God that we tend to overlook the essence of what is the Bible where the Bible was written. If we was to at least take a few moments of our time every day and just meditate on scripture and ask The Holy Spirit to open our spiritual eye, on how our Jewish brothers, and how God's gospel has exploded in such a supernatural way, and how it came to us, because, the Salvation originally, came for the Jews, and God is so merciful, and so loving, and kind, that he gave it,(the Bible) to us, through the Jews. Which you know pretty much, God gave them the knowledge, and how they were supposed to give us the knowledge as well. And I do not think God favored anyone in any type of way. I just believe that God chose these people to make an example for the whole world to see. What it is to be under a Supreme being or what it is to have a divine way of life, and how they live their lives according to scripture and how they separate themselves from any type of contamination from the world. Thus, how they consistently are following God's laws and consistently following God's rules and constantly learning and how they are constantly praying, and fasting, and they keep God's festivals, and that is, what you would call a model of what a citizen of heaven is. So, when I started contemplating that. I am like wow! God literally brought the Jewish people and made them a model on earth. Which is what is being done in heaven, and it just mind blowing. How a Christians mentality ignores that way of visualizing the actions of the Jews. Not realizing how the enemy has them only thinking of their wants and needs, a selfish train of thought and not even worrying about what God wants for us. I place myself in that category at one point in my life until I Realized that was wrong way of thinking. God hates selfishness and proud people. It is in the Bible and how we so easily follow worldly traditions and worldly festivals. Which the Bible really condemn that practice and how it speaks totally against it. Yet, they continue to practice these things. So, if you really put your mind to it, and understand the concept of how Israel is so important in our lives, how we should be keeping up to date with Israel and how we should keep praying and fasting and studying the word and asking the Lord to please take care of Israel and bless Israel and protect Israel. Israel is where we are going to live even though the new Jerusalem is going to be sent from heaven down to earth that is in the Bible. You know what I am literally trying to explain to you the reader is that this is so crucial, and this is so important for you to understand that Israel is your Homeland. Israel, is where you will serve the Lord forever and ever an where you will walk the streets of gold and see the seas of glass and have a home where you do not have to pay light, water, gas, etc. etc. You will have the Messiah with you, 24/7 where we will be able to speak to Angels and they will speak to us and speak to people that were saved with us, and it is going to be in Jerusalem. If you cannot fathom what gift is being placed in our hands. I'm trying to make you understand, this is so crucial and so important that you make this part of your life that you put it in place in your heart for Israel and you put it place in your mind with the Jewish people that they had been decades and years and years always been ridiculed and always attacked and always been criticized and hurt, and us being Christian and being in the United states that God has blessed us in so many ways to where we can actually live in a place, where we're not being tortured or not being attacked or not being surrounded by enemies and how we must constantly be asking the Lord to protect Israel is something so important. Doing this will show the Lord, that you do love his people, why because, we are his people as well, we are injected into Israel, so we are the spiritual Israelites which is something so amazing. That our Lord chose us to be part of Israel and if we were to really think that way we can see and feel that every time we read a story on how they were attacked and how their children were killed and how all these horrific events came to be and place ourselves in that suffering we can utterly understand the Jewish people. Therefore, we can put a closeness with them because we too as well, have had events in our lives that are so emotional hard and overwhelming that it makes us feel tremendous suffering, so could you imagine being a people that are constantly being chased out of countries that were constantly being persecuted, do not forget the six million Jews that died in the Holocaust. Still to this day, there are Jewish people that lived in those days and now they are older elders and how they can still remember, like it was yesterday. I think that is such a horrific thing to live by and how God has kept them strong. I always wish that God would awaken a lot of our believers' brothers and sisters of the faith to give more love and more understanding and to try to learn more about Israel's culture and the festival's because it is part of who we are as well. You see the minute we accept the Lord Jesus Christ in our life, we also accept Israel. We also accepted to be become citizens of Israel and spiritual citizens and ambassadors of Heaven. So, we also accepted their festivals, we accepted there way of life. That is what God wants us to do. God does not want you to continue living a selfish or a hypocritical life of saying OK, now, I am a Christian, so now, I do not think sinful , any longer. I am aware of God, but I can continue to practice the same things, I did before, I chose to serve God. No way! Jose! That is not a full redemption. Redemption is when you learn to accept that you are putting God and his word, First. Thus, you are expected to learn from Israel. You are expected to learn from their biblical teachings, that you are expected to become a spiritual Israelite, then you will see the difference between a regular commitment to a religious belief, to where it is a supernatural commitment. Everything has a commitment whether it be a job, whether it be anything that you put your mind to, you must commit to it, just like any author must commit to constantly spending hours and hours of research and investigating, you know, things that you are studying or researching. So, if you really put your mind with the Holy Spirit and let him guide, you will see that there is a lot more than what the Christian understanding is being taught on earth. I mean there is more to the Bible. There is more to a supernatural living is more to festivals of God. So, we are to even fathom to even worry about anything else. At the end of the day, what are They the Jewish people doing, there waiting for the redemption, there waiting for God to take them to a new World? Israel is waiting for a renewal of World through the waiting of their Messiah. The Church is waiting for the gathering or rapture, the great gathering of people that have given their lives to God and put their lives as a way of life and studying and fasting and going to services and congregating. But, there is a deeper understanding if you become the actual essence of having the Holy Spirit help you understand or guide you to understand that you are more than just a Christian, you are a child of God you see I say the child of God, is something that I believe it has more depth in it more understanding it's more profound it gives you more of a deeper sense that you know. You are not just any type of child, you are a child of God, a child of God's a lot of blessings and, also has a lot of rules and regulations that the Bible has stated that you must follow to come to the Kingdom of heaven. You see many Christians brothers and sisters always are saying avoid sin that we must move away from sin. yeah, that is exactly what Israel does 24/7 every day a week of course there's people in Israel that do not follow the bible, you know, they just want to live their lives daily, feed their kids, work etc. etc. you also have those that are just basically committing their lives to living a Christian Kingdom living life. Now just focus on what I just said a **Christian Kingdom living life,** what is a Christian Kingdom living life, is that you are a Christian, you are waiting for the Kingdom, that is about to come, and you are practicing on earth for the Kingdom that is coming! Remember the Prayer Yahshua (Jesus)taught to those who did not know how to pray Our Father who art in heaven hallowed be thy name thy Kingdom come. Now if you put that in in mind you understand this is a Kingdom that is coming it is not here yet. If you look at Israel, you see how they live their lives daily and how they are constantly reading the Bible, also, another thing, constantly, teaching their children of the Bible and that is why they have the ceremony of bar mitzvahs for their sons, after a certain age. When there sons hit the age of 13 they are considered to be in the stage of knowing sin and they are being accountable at that age,you see even at that time the jewish parents are preparing there male sons to know God and to accept there upcoming time of adulthood and commitment with their God, all these things have more in-depth spiritual understanding, they (the Jewish people) are constantly practicing the festivals of God, remember, I said before, there not festivals of the Jews, their festivals of God. The Almighty ordained it to all who believe in him it is in Deuteronomy the Old Testament. Look for it, read it, and you know if you do not want to believe me prove me wrong! but it is in the Bible. Know, in my own personal experience, I have seen that every time, I have practiced Yom Kippur, Hanukkah, Passover, I received nothing, but a blessing in my spiritual life, family members, that have practiced it with me friends I have invited they had said, that it felt so supernatural that they felt that Jesus was there, and I said, he was. So, can you imagine, how in Israel knows what they are doing, and how these festivals give them a higher meaning, gives them more knowledge of what the festival's mean and how God took them out of depression, and how God took him out of oppression and out of slavery. We ourselves can benefit also, by having knowledge of how Israel lives their lives and how Israel is so important in a Christian’s life. Whether you are a Christian or just a believer in the word of God it does not really matter. whether you know of what type of denomination you are, now there is so many denominations of Christian Systems In the world. I always say that it is so better to call yourself a child of God then call yourself a Christian. Well, that is just my opinion, does not necessarily mean it is bad to be called a Christian. I'm just saying it has more meaning when you call yourself a child of God then say your denominations and there's so many different aspects of what the Bible is, or what the Bible means, there's so many derogatory teachings from different types of Christian ministries I just say that if you say you're a child of God ,you don't segregate and you don't separate yourself from your faith brothering, if not you just create a unity it's a word of unity, a word of one body, with your fellow brothers of the faith. I believe that's so important to grasp the knowledge that you are a child of God you belong to the Kingdom of heaven that's why the Bible says that this world will not know you and will hate you because it does not love God so any type of misunderstanding that you expect just because you're a Christian that people should love you or respect you because you follow God the Bible states it's not going to happen but other people are going to hate you. Why, because the world is under the demonic influence of Satan himself in the end dominions and all the evil in the Sky that you do not see. suddenly most of the people that do not follow God or constantly just following the devil's plan its simple, I am not sugarcoating I am just speaking truth so if you think Israel is important or not let the Holy Spirit reveal that to you. Israel is important and we should all love Israel all those that declare that God is their savior should all in their right minds love Israel and pray for Israel and get to know Israel's culture get to know Yahweh's festivals then you will see that the Holy Spirit will reveal a whole brand-new understanding of what the true gospel of Christ really is.

Conclusion

I hope this book gives you an insight on how important it is to know these Festivals of God and how important they should be part of our lives. These festivals are of God, given to us by God, and Mandated to assemble and practice these Festivals because, they are from God. These Festivals should be in the Churches and not worldly Festivals that have nothing to do with God. These are his festivals and are yours as well. All we must do is listen to the Holy Spirit. HE will guide you and give you a better understanding of what these Festivals have to offer to every child of God. It is a blessing and a way of showing true devotion to your Creator and Messiah Our Lord Yahshua (Jesus Christ). So, with, I hope you enjoyed this small touch of knowledge and an understanding that these festivals also belong to you. Given by our Lord and God to his children on earth. May the blessings of God come upon you every day of your life and your loved ones Always. Sincerely from your brother in Christ, thank you for your time, I hope this book gives you an understanding of who you are in Gods eyes and what you mean to him. Shalom and God Bless.

www.ingramcontent.com/pod-product-compliance
Lightning Source LLC
LaVergne TN
LVHW052053160826
845678LV00015B/3201

9798504281162